Why Elephants No Longer Communicate in Greek

Why Elephants No Longer Communicate in Greek

poems

Timons Esaias

Concrete Wolf
Louis Award Series

Why Elephants No Longer Communicate in Greek
Copyright ©2016 Timons Esaias

All rights reserved. No part of this publication may be reproduced, distributed or transmitted in any form or by any means whatsoever without written permission from the publisher, except in the case of brief excerpts for critical reviews and articles. All inquiries should be addressed to Concrete Wolf Press.

Concrete Wolf Louis Award Series

FIRST EDITION

Printed in the United States of America

ISBN 978-0-9964754-1-9

Cataloging Information: 1. Esaias, Timons, 1954; 2. Contemporary American Poetry.

Book design: Tonya Namura using Baskerville and Teutonic No1.

Cover art: Loxodonta Libro by Ethan Hahn, pencil, 2015.

Rook illustrations: courtesy of St. Louis artist Sheila Harris.

Author photo: Ruth E. Hendricks.

The Concrete Wolf Louis Award Series honors poets over age 50 who have not yet published a full-length collection of poems.

Concrete Wolf
PO Box 1808
Kingston, WA 98346

http://ConcreteWolf.com

ConcreteWolfPress@gmail.com

Acknowledgements

The rook illustrations are courtesy of St. Louis artist Sheila Harris, my sister-in-law.

I wish to thank and acknowledge the publications in which many of these poems first appeared: *5AM (2)*, *Abandoned Towers*, *Alembic*, *Asimov's Science Fiction (4)*, *Atlanta Review* (title poem), *Bathtub Gin (3)*, *Elysian Fields Quarterly (2)*, *Eskimo Pie*, *Fantasy Commentator*, *hotmetalpoets.com*, *Loyalhanna Review*, *Magazine of Speculative Poetry (3)*, *Main Street Rag (3)*, *NewMyths.com*, *Nexus*, *Pavement Saw (2)*, *Pittsburgh Poetry Review*, *Polu Texni*, *Pulp (5)*, *Reflections*, *Rune*, *Santa Clara Review*, *Ship of Fools (4)*, *star*line (2)*, *Tales of the Unanticipated*, *Terra Incognita*, *The Brentwood Anthology*, *The Influence of Pigeons on Architecture (12)*, *tomorrowsf*, *Uppagus (4)*, *Willard & Maple*, and *yawp (2)*.

Thanks are also due to these anthologies and other markets, which reprinted several of these poems: *2001: A Science Fiction Poetry Anthology*, *Alexandria Digital Literature (3)*, *Along These Rivers (2)*, *DVP Anthology*, *Stories About Time*, *The Brentwood Anthology (5)*, and *The Rhysling Anthology (2)*.

Special thanks to Mike James and his Yellow Pepper Press, for publishing my chapbook *The Influence of Pigeons on Architecture*.

I want to express my gratitude to two critique groups – The Worldwrights (of the Mary Soon Lee era) and Pittsburgh Poetry Exchange – which worked to improve many of the pieces in this collection; and likewise to Calie Voorhis.

"The Four-Fold Path" was written in memory of two colleagues, Jack Wolford and Flonet Biltgen.

Finally, the existence of this book is rooted in my first published poem, written for my 8th grade Language Arts teacher (and great friend), Peggy Usher.

for Bernadette

&

*to anyone
now & forever
living
through the
word*

"The elephant...in intelligence approaches the nearest to man. It understands the language of its country, ...and it remembers all the duties which it has been taught. It is a well-known fact, that one of these animals, who was slower than usual in learning what was taught him, and had been frequently chastised with blows, was found conning over his lesson in the night-time... Mutianus, who was three times consul, informs us that one of these animals had been taught to trace the Greek letters, and that he used to write in that language..."

—Pliny, *Naturalis Historiæ*, Book VIII

Table of Contents

I

All The Important People #5	5
It Only Takes One	6
BS Detector Reading Off The Scale	7
Things I'm Tired of Excusing	8
Newton's Mass	10
here	11
The Blank Bits	13
All The Important People #2	15
My Movie	16
An Amendment	18
The Four-Fold Path	19
Robbed!	20
On Not Opening That Box, Ever Again	22
Eight Iniquities	24
Some Days It Drives Me Nuts	26
Supplementary	27
Checklist	29
We Used To Have Faces	31
Numbered	32
By Their Sidewalks You Will Know Them	33
Why Elephants No Longer Communicate in Greek	35
Russians in the Produce Aisle	37
de angeli	38
Why Elephants No Longer Communicate in Greek #2	40
All The Important People #1	41
Red Beans, Rice	42

II

All Day I Waited	47
A Fire on Ganymede	48
Conversion	50
inquest	51
Six Leaves on Shaded Elm	52

A Universe	53
All The Important People #6	54
Please Note	55
Hello	57
Looking at This Streetscape	59
The Influence of Pigeons on Architecture	60
Do They Still Pick Rags in My Old City?	62
Even the Crippled	63
Sentinels	64
At Monteverdi's *Magnificat*	65
Carnegie Library, Pittsburgh	67
The Van	68
Domain	69
Like an Old War Horse	70
Commandments for July	71
No Solicitors #1	73
customer parking only	74
Squirrel Hill, Saturday	76
A Break for Freedom in the 61C Cafe	77
Superman Behind the Counter	78
All The Important People #7	79
Nature, Suffering by Comparison	80
Insidious	81
Armageddon	83
On Visiting the Dying Suburban Mall	84
It's All Time-Machines, She Said	85

III

For Love, This Cup	89
Stipulated Conditions	90
Postulate #5	92
The Origin of a Long, Bitter Story	93
Follies	94
Hair	96
Awkward Stage	97
Would I Give the World, All of It, for Love?	98
93 Lines Wasted	99

What I Learned	103
What She Was	104
In The Whole History Of Time?	106
The Progressive	107
Eyes, This Big	108
Family	109
"But will they come when you do call for them?"	110
Photonic Relationships	112
Not For Love, But Something Else	114

IV

Lines Written to an Unknown Audience, Waiting for the Night's First Act	117
The Alcoholic Beverages of India	118
Not Feeling That Lucky, Seeking	120
New Labels on Old Jars	122
Famous Poet, Rant, Point of Order	123
At the Mountain Inn, Shaded by Broken Pines	127
14 Lines	129
In Each of Our Wallets	130
Nudge	132
Deadline	133
in kiva han	135
The Latest Literary Device	136
Poetry Defined	138
I Really Think Sela Ward Should Have Dropped the String of Pearls and the Coral Lipstick and the Whole Suburban Goddess Shtick and Gone with Sheer Glamour and *Femme Fatale*, Infuriating Other Women and Turning Men into Slavering Puddles of Meaningless Meat; but This Poem Isn't about Her Anyway	139
You Must Not Be Taken In	142
Rubaiyat LXXI, Revised	143
My Play	144
Linguistic Changes to Look For	145
Cogmire	146

To Demur	147
Appropriate Salutations	148
Concise Credo	149
About the Author	151

Why Elephants No Longer Communicate in Greek

I

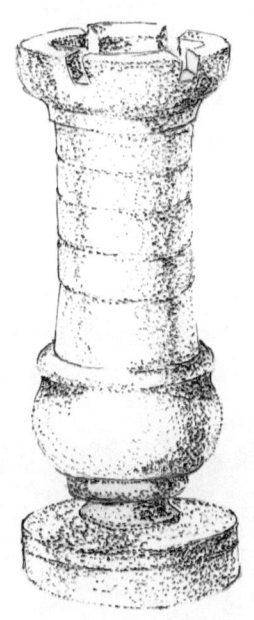

All The Important People #5

I looked for an oracle, o Master,
to riddle the koan of
bell tower breed dog foreign city
turned to the Internet and behold
my search ended with a prophet's words
Joseph Smith of the golden tablets
speaking to the saints at Navoo
telling them that Zion is the Americas
though I had thought it to be Jerusalem
and would be guarded by Cherubim
grim as mastiffs, and I know
there is a bell tower in there somewhere
but I get lost among the twelve olive trees
and the twelve stakes
and start wondering why people trust
golden tablets that no-one lets them see
and my search has brought me to a prophecy
given to a famous audience
but I understand nothing
see only suspect words on a page.

It Only Takes One

It only takes one really
good lie
to get the truth off your back.

Just insist, for instance, that
the Earth
is merely an over-elaborate metaphor.

Just insist, for instance, that before
the Goddess
we were immortal and all this is a muddled dream.

Just insist, for instance, that
true freedom
is found only in flagrant falsehood.

Just do that, and they won't
argue much,
but will sputter and fume and leave you alone.

Just lie, and stick to it,
and physics,
responsibility, even fact, can take no hold.

BS Detector Reading Off The Scale

It troubles me that the
kabalists and the
cosmologists
work from the same list of
possibilities.

Everything
from a slight change in the Void,
or from an egg,
or a steady state,
or boom and bust.

It troubles me that the
kabalists and the
cosmologists
come to the same
conclusions

And both think their
numbers work.

Things I'm Tired of Excusing

I am tired of starships that go whoosh in space
and fighters that bank through turns in vacuum
and any device in the future that doesn't
automatically
assess the value of reversing the polarity.

I am tired of accepting your ignorance
as the excuse
for the crap they feed me.

That goes double for stock market reports
that pretend the market "tries" to do
this and "wants" to do anything
as though it had a will
and politicians who pretend
that more is ever done
with less.

I am tired of pretending that
cooking dinner somehow fails
to heat the planet, tired
of the idea that we can
do things without consequences
tired of being told that nothing
can be done because you
the public
are not ready.

Get ready.

I am truly tired of hearing that your ignorance
is why I listen to lies
all day long.

Newton's Mass

How the pine tree came to be
integral to Newton's birthday
is unclear.

One would expect, from legend,
an apple tree; or an ash,
for Yggdrasill, that his theories
replaced.

Whatever the reason, fitting,
that families gravitate
on this day of remembrance
to its evergreen.

Fitting, the delicate orbs
we hang on it, evoking planets,
evoking the undone crystalline
spheres.

Fitting, the way the ornaments
divide and play with the light,
and also the day, coming so soon
after the increasing of it.

Fitting, the season
revolves about money,
for he was
Master of the Mint.

here

The menu here
in the coffee shop
tells you everything but
what a simple, plain
mug of coffee
costs,
just as the world
tells you all kinds of things
but obscures the issue
of what living in it
costs,
as my aunt tells you everything
about everything
in her church
and her town
except what spending her time
talking about their petty
selfish
hypocritical lives
costs her
in spirit and in hope,
and as certain women offer their attention
and anything else
except a specific bill of particulars
yet mercilessly exile to the streets
and bawdy houses those of their sisters
who are willing to quote a fixed
price
for particular, somewhat limited, services
but even there surprises may await

in the long-term
price
department – but here
in this coffee shop
they're taking the first step
toward those exclusive restaurants where
there is no
price
for anything listed
which gives the signal
that if you need to know the
cost
then you don't belong here,
which is also what life
is really like,
because we do,
but we're here.

The Blank Bits

Okay, here's what I'm afraid of:
it's those blank spaces in the DNA
where there isn't a gene
and we have no idea what
all those repetitions mean.

Because what I'm afraid of
is finding out that the blank spaces,
the junk DNA, are the essence
of some ancient bacterium, or some virus
that invaded an ancestral cell
and directed our evolution solely
for its unicellular gratification.

Because what I'm afraid of
is that all this time we,
all the animals, all the plants,
yea, even the fungi, have just
been huge organic battlebots
encasing the latest incarnations
of some vermin who neither knows
nor cares what he's created
as long as it doesn't interfere
with his current, limited, mindless
needs.

And when I think about my relation
to society, civilization, the Zeitgeist,
that each of us helps constitute
and none of us much affirms or

admits to, well, then
what I realize I'm afraid of
is something like myself.

All The Important People #2

Much is lost. My age. Who
that woman in the yellow chair is.
If it's Tuesday that we have hot-dogs
or another day.

Lethe is a word that I remember. I keep
dreaming that a Saint Bernard with
one of those little kegs, brought me
water from Lethe.

I am afraid. That woman is afraid, too.
Questions keep coming, mysteries, threats,
and that is frightening, and so also
is dreaming.

I have only fragments. A bell tower;
the name of a city in what I think is Europe;
all the important people, nameless now,
gathered at my wedding.

My Movie

Okay, first scene:
character is by a river
sees Charon, rowing across
the Styx, or is it Acheron?,
look it up,
anyway out of the sky,
if it's sky in the underworld,
so, let's say
out of the gloom
comes this Jap Zero,
strafes the boat,
and behind it comes a Henschel,
one of those tank busters
with the cannon in the nose
don't know the type (plane)
or caliber (cannon),
look it up,
and it strafes, too.

Charon sinks.

Character wonders meaning.
Okay, World War Two,
they were allies,
but what sense does this make?
And what happens with everybody,
er, everyspirit, that is,
backing up on the near shore?

And why is this happening today,
decades after the war?

An Amendment

Since the guardians of our liberty have proposed
to protect the Flag
by desecrating the Constitution,

I propose to approve the idea;
but I would say: Be precise.
For the Flag should be inviolate,
even Constitutionally protected:
but only in those moments when it is serving
as a wind-gauge
in a National League Baseball Park,
during a game,
for only then
is it truly sacred.

The Four-Fold Path

The thing is not to cling
too tightly
to this sphere.

Plan, always,
for a quick release.

And don't scuff it up
too much
before you let it go.

Add nothing,
do nothing,
that would offend
an umpire.

Robbed!

> *"Kill the Umpire!*
> *But Torture Him First!!"*
> T-shirt slogan

The replay proves the truth; our plaint is just,
The last out ours; – of comfort, no man speak: instead
Let's talk of graves, of worms, and epitaphs;
Make infield clay our paper, and with rainy eyes
Write sorrow on the bosom of the field.
Let's choose lawyers, and threaten suits:
And yet not so, – for what can we win back,
That blots out this entry in the record books?
Our lands, our lives, and all are Baseball's,
And nothing can we call our own but teams,
And that small mound of barren earth
Which serves as paste and center to our games.
For God's sake, let us sit upon the bench,
And tell cruel stories of the death of umpires: –
How some have been struck blind by righteous fans;
Some choked with marking chalk; some slain with bats;
Some haunted by the calls they clearly blew;
Some poison'd for their faults; some sleeping kill'd;
All call'd out: – for within the hollow mask
That rounds the mortal temples of an ump
Keeps Death his box; and there the antic sits,
Scoffing his state, and grinning at his pomp;
Allowing him a breath, a little scene,
To monarchize, be fear'd, and twist the rules;
Infusing him with self and vain conceit, –
As if that flesh, which hangs over his belt,

Were brass impregnable; and humor'd thus,
Comes at the last, and with a little pin
Bores through his outfield-wall, and farewell, ump.

On Not Opening That Box, Ever Again

Small, it is in another box
for a reason
and, for a reason,
I'm not sure which one.

In the airport
they took my life
apart
except for the tiny boxes
containing nothing.
They were looking for
what wasn't there,
and those little boxes
were full of just that,
but they lost interest.

I had a leaf
from Troy.

The lost box should be ignored.
It should not be discovered
by kin, or by enemies,
least of all by me.
I sometimes wish it held
a secret,
scandalous,
but it doesn't.

I should have been flattered
that I was such a
threat.

Like when I was told
I was wrong for her,
which has a nice ring
to it.
Wrong for her.

The leaf was an oak leaf.

I waited at the Temples of
Karnak for a long time.
She didn't come.

The family who raised this menhir,
a small clan,
did not know the Egyptians.
They would not have ignored
the leaf.

Looking for what is not there
can take a long time.
It may be wrong for you.

Eight Iniquities

You ask what the Great Sins are,
a good question,
and certainly visiting Boston yet
not at least walking by the *Constitution*
would qualify.

Not eating clam chowder
when in Maine.

Manhattan clam chowder
is a sin in itself;
and another is like unto it:
tomato aspic.

Not buying a ticket
when the lottery exceeds seventy million dollars
is impious
though not a sin.

Beginning any day
without a beignet
is a common, almost unavoidable
dereliction,
remitted by sighing, regretfully
in the direction
of Jackson Square, twice daily,
for which a mihrab
is suggested.

To think that one can only love
when one can explain
is error. Likewise not standing,
once, in the Sacred Precinct
of the Pythian Apollo. Likewise
avoiding Ise or Kamakura or Anglesey.

To fail in alms to one's local library
is abomination; to not see Istanbul
almost as great. To throw away
a loved teddy bear, Greatest of all.

Some Days It Drives Me Nuts

Given a button
for happiness
we are told, a rat
will just keep pushing it
languish to keep pushing it
starve to keep pushing it
die pushing it
and so would we
seems the lesson
but the surprise is
that so many don't,
instead find pressing reasons to
put it off for a more auspicious day
a calmer period
when the kids are grown
or the mortgage paid
or the product shipped
or for some highly-touted outsider
to come and decide for them
whether they deserve it
and some days it drives me nuts
and I just want to stand
on the corner
screaming
"Push the button, for crying out loud;
just push the
goddam
button."

Supplementary

The element actinium is, I assume,
the chemical basis of all action,
just as selenium is the element necessary
for appreciation of the Moon, and iron the element
that allows us to press clean laundry into
crisp sharp folds.

I have questions. Questions about the absence
of people lining up for actinium, or does the lack
itself ensure a measure of apathy? Questions about
the multi-vitamins that have iron for laundry,
selenium for romance, zinc for doing dishes,
but no actinium, no samarium for kindness to strangers
     on the road,
no hafnium to let us find contentment
with less than the whole.
What good was isolating the building blocks
of our nature, of naming the elements,
then leaving the hard-won knowledge all unused?

Where are the specialized supplements? Thorium
for carpenters and others who hammer all day long?
Where the lutetium for guitarists and players of strings;
or, for architects, that they might value
the formal and elegant, the palladium?
And for those who mourn, yearning to heal through tears,
why no Niobium anywhere to be had?

Likewise, I query the absence of regulations
suppressing Californium – for reasons that need not

be enumerated – or keeping Promethium out of the hands
of arsonists. And further, I wonder,
if the world might be more unified, more tolerant,
without the intoxication with Western values
brought on by excessive Europium
in human diet; and I debate whether we need more,
or less, of the element behind nostalgia:
argon.

Perhaps those in positions to decide
fear the consequences of too much Nobelium
and far too few Prizes; of too many on Lawrencium
and not enough Arabia to conquer.

I see their point, for
how I would love to book flight
to Jidda, take a few pills
and find myself riding
with the Jazi Howeitat, to free the tribes
from whatever it is that they need
freeing from just now; yes, campaigning
with the Sharifs, but for enough
Lawrencium, and the regular minimum
daily requirement
of actinium.

Checklist

How many arms are best?
I pondered. How many arms does a
modern man need?

ARMS: ? the form inquired.

Six seemed wise; a click.
Another click for neural implants to
Drive them.

What SKIN COLOR: should I choose?
A question shackled with symbolism
Rich in cultural significance.
My ancestors painted themselves blue
from head to toe
blue
When they faced momentous possibility:
War
and death.

I scrolled SELECTION to
OTHER.
Inserted WOAD BLUE.

INSIGNIA: ? it asked next, HERALDRY ?
One holo-icon in the palm of each hand
A thunderbolt, for the weather lately tamed
A flame, for fusion harnessed and made slave
A shield, to note our meteor defense

A circle of beads, as symbol of our endless string of days
A Khadga mace, for the power true self-knowledge gave
And finally,
A sword, to mark the division from error,
from Aristotle's broken, insufficient tool;
My hands a celebration of the March of Man;
of *Homo sapiens autotransfigurans*.

My first day out
sensations still deliciously new,
Scars healed,
Drinking thé kurdique on the Boulevard St-Michel
A couple, passing, frankly admiring
My new aspect and attributes.

Are we not become gods?
She asked him.
Are we not become gods?

We Used To Have Faces

They were the reward
of character, of sustaining selves
through long hard hauls of
lifetimes. Not the fat-slicked,
temple-tucked, botoxed
visages we have now. The
only-seen-the-outside-on-vacations,
barbecues, and tennis lessons
blank slates.

The weather-beaten among us
play golf.

Booze still helps, or heroin.
Madness sometimes etches
an interesting image
on a hapless head;
but addiction, madness,
is not character; though
modern cattle-people
mistake the wreckage
for something more;
admire it, romanticize it,
for, at least,
those people still have faces.

Numbered

I wish to be numbered
among those
who came.

There will be no time
for explanation
the being here
is the meaning
is the long story
in a single act.

Our differences
are many, but
number me with you.

History will make
my name smoke
will not know
the couch I rose from
the possessions that the
enemy will ransack.

Here I am.
Count me
among the rest
this time
with you.

By Their Sidewalks You Will Know Them

Originally there were eleven Commandments.
Moses, perhaps confused by the unfamiliar
snow, *ice*, and *sidewalk*,
botched one, and left it out.

But Buddha said that though Life is Pain,
falling on ice is gratuitous pain,
and those who cause it, by neglect,
should never escape the Wheel of Rebirth;
and Lao-Tzu agreed, for those who will not
clear the path will never find the Way.

Zoroaster, in the endless war of light
against ice, demanded diligence;
claimed that those who surrender
the public way to the Enemy
have empty souls,
can scarcely be regarded as human.

The Prophet, regarding sidewalks and snow,
is silent; but his sura
Sand Drifting Against the Caravanserai Gate
is thought to apply. The condemnation there
is brutal and eternal.

Plato counted safe sidewalks as fundamental
to the ideal Republic, noting that those remiss
in this clear duty lacked all character;

and his pupil – perceptive, immortal Aristotle –
further declared, famously, that
lack of character
is destiny.

Why Elephants No Longer Communicate in Greek

We seem to have asked them
nothing.

Elephants once shared our lives,
fought our enemies, battered down
city gates, carried great burdens,
headed the tiger hunts,
which protected us both,
howdahs teeming with spearmen and archers.

And in the reign of Titus Augustus
elephants were known to have mastered
Latin, and the brightest ones
Greek.

Yet we asked them nothing,
heeded nothing.

No scholar recorded, that we know,
their preferences in reading. Did elephants favor
Aristotle over Cicero? The Stoics, or,
with their great appetites, the Epicureans?
Did they care for drama, master Euclid,
penetrate the numbers of Pythagoras?
Clearly we did not pay attention, did not
record the year in which the elephants
were no longer writing Greek, or even note it.

Much has opened to us since the plow first broke
furrows back and forth across the ground
but other doors have closed to us.
Delphi is still, the gods
no longer speak to us,
and the elephants have, inexplicably,
put their pens aside.

Russians in the Produce Aisle

I spent half my life thinking
the Berlin Wall would never
come down.
These students are stunned
to learn Russia
was in the Cold War.

I tell them
about the Russian immigrants
in the produce aisle.
Frozen by choices, frozen
by fear.

Not just the pounds and ounces
instead of grams and roubles.
But the wrongness of food
on the same side of the wall
as the customers.
But the thoughtlessness
of not telling
how many you can try to buy
without being arrested.

For them, the heads of lettuce
were a minefield.
Everything in that aisle
was tempting, and terrifying
and very wrong.

It said Danger.
Danger.

de angeli

Reading Aquinas
on angels
one sees he was
really defining photons.

Creatures of pure light
outside the realm of time
weightless, in their natural state,
traveling in true straight lines,
which only inadequate perception
our limited point of view
sees as curved, or bent.

They can carry messages.
When they fall
there is perceptible impact
despite the absence
of mass.
And there is heat.
They end in heat.

Any number may visit
the head of a pin
simultaneously
but Aquinas fails to mention
that the pin might melt.

He resisted the notion
that there could be
too many true messages.

That there could be
too much light.

Why Elephants No Longer Communicate in Greek #2

When I was young, I learned this:
Symbols, and the books
one builds from them
let thoughts travel in time;
let the dead, or distant,
speak to me,
personally.

Now old, I think on this:
Pliny's and Plutarch's
elephants,
trying so hard, burning
the midnight oil
over their lessons.

Trying so very hard.

All The Important People #1

I almost took it up today,
this book, this great and noble book,
(that I won't name, but imagine
War and Peace or *A Research Report
on Misplaced Time*) yes, I
almost took it up, but lay
instead, idle, upon the porch
wondering why intelligence partakes
too little of wisdom; and if self-delusion
is a waste of tithe and life, is money
the only real substitute?
All the important people have crossed the St. Bernard
and gone down to Florence
for the Campanile, have read this famous book,
and know the author's dates.
All the important people
are living the lives I meant to have,
but can't quite muster.

Red Beans, Rice

Today I am ignoring Pythagoras.
Don't get me wrong, he was right
about so much, about numbers, dead right,
more than almost anyone understands.
But on the subject of beans,
the necessity to avoid,
Pythagoras is best looked upon
with charity.

Today I am spending the day
with beans. One pot red beans;
the other pot a diversity,
eight varieties grown in my garden
the seventy square feet of boxed earth
parked on my city-lot driveway.
They are soaked in wine
flavored with salt pork, buried in onions,
anointed with oil,
the eight kinds and the one kind.

It's an all-day job,
an eight hour shift,
to cook them down,
snatching quarter-hours to
write this poem to you,
and a story later; quarter-hours
between stirring, though
toward the end, as in
any good alchemy,
they will require constant attention

lest the heavenly concoction burn
and be cast into the trash pit
forever.

A day, eight hours,
and then one more hour
to cool down, before they are
poured into crockery
and refrigerated.
All this time for a side dish.
Inefficient, a massive waste of
energy and time, or so it looks
on paper, and so Pythagoras might
argue, but neither assessment
penetrates the mystery, explains
why friends are heard to ask
in my hearing, if it is not perhaps
too long since
I made beans.

Religions use the metaphors
of fermentation, bread and wine, metaphors
of cooking, and then claim these
reflect underlying spiritual truths.
It is a lie.
The underlying truth is that
their analogies are stolen
from the real miracles
of the kitchen, are pious
hopes that something about us

will mirror the transformation
I will achieve today, with these
eight hours and the one,
turning simple ingredients into ambrosia,
drawing people to my table
not for a communion that is *like* communion,
but for communion that *is* communion.

Common garlic and household pepper sauce
already simmer in the formula.
In a few hours I will sprinkle in
salt, mined from the earth,
the rediscovered remnants of an ancient sea.

II

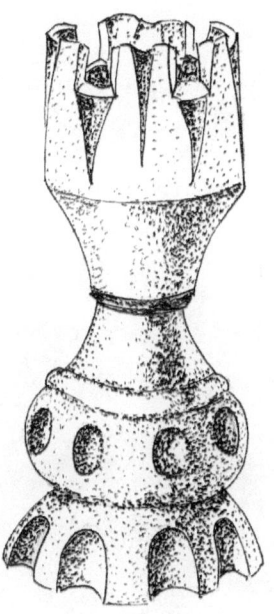

All Day I Waited

All day I waited, for the scoop
from Mars;
for the promised press conference:
the first geology, first spectroscopy,
first sight of Deimos from below,
the Monster Pan.

The wonders of technology brought down these
treasures from Sojourner to Pathfinder to Earth
to JPL to CNN to TCI
but with, at last,
the Grail of knowledge almost at my lips
it slipped away.

TV ran commercials
through the spectroscopy,
commercials
through the geology,
promised to go back to the pictures but
"let's bring in so-and-so for her reaction"
because in America we cherish talk, talk, talk;
talk above everything;
opinions without data;

and obliterate wonderful pictures
with a thousand futile words.

A Fire on Ganymede

You cannot build a fire
on Ganymede,
gather the deadwood
and work up a pleasant sweat
chopping and splitting.
You cannot sit around the campfire
afterwards, making awful coffee
in a pan, telling impossible lies
about how unique your own past has been.
You cannot breathe in the bitter wood-smoke
on Ganymede,
the product of inefficient oxidation,
you cannot, that is, pollute the air
and not care because it is so pleasant,
and say to yourself I will not think
about how horrible it would be if all
the galaxy's billions were indulging
in a campfire
at once, and gee what's next, anyway?
Yes, you cannot have that problem
on Ganymede
because you can't have a campfire there
and so, frankly, one might as well
not go.

Now there is
undoubtedly
some fine reason or another to see
the place, and it's probably
all right for some

city-bred bristle-head who
has never seen the outside
of a mall.
Send *them* to find the undoubtedly
superior pleasures
of Ganymede
but leave us old codgers alone.
We have no time for it,
we know better, we have
our standards.

And don't even ask me what the Buddha
would have urged
about detachment and divorcing the ego
from the material.
When Buddha lived, everyone
burned wood, or dung, or
charcoal
for all their fires, every day.
The smoke hung everywhere,
he wouldn't have been able
to get away from it,
and I'll bet, when he finally
left the world of illusion,
finally got free,
he felt it missing
and briefly
regretted it.

Conversion

Down in the plains, the prayers
turned into stone. Sometimes
into running blood.

Above the trees, the prayers became wind,
kites, smoke. Sometimes
bodies were laid out
as prayers.

In the karst, great holes
filled with prayers. Sometimes
there was a way to follow
and still come back. Sometimes
whole rivers took the prayers
with them,
and disappeared.

On the sea, the waves.

inquest

at some point the
paychecks didn't come
so the wind,
demoralized, went from soft
to languid to intermittent
and finally stopped.

the Gulf Stream
stayed in Florida
hoarding its energy,
lived off-shore to
avoid taxes and rent.

osmosis just didn't.

crystals stood first
at ease
then broke ranks.

Six Leaves on Shaded Elm

Six leaves on shaded elm
                        And he
a Faëry castle to the bee

Gargantuan tower to the ants
    countless generations building
Reverent from misty ages past.

Huge and old and solid still
Reaching far into darkened sky
Vaulted edge of Universe far above him
He dies.

Caernarvon of wood.

Home of Nations, wasp, ant, bee
But having failed to touch the sky
He, like all towers, failed.

Babel of insects.

A Universe

Properly, it should be
seductive
– repay all the
trouble
of perception.

It should have no
beginning, must
at the very start
be already in
motion;
and no end.

Its theme should be accessible.

Whether it should have Time
is a question;
the pathos
and Death, its companion,
so often betray
poor taste.

Properly, it should
resonate
– clear; like all the
bells ever cast,
intertwined,
purified.

All The Important People #6

The bell implied
bell tower
he said
but really a cat
belled
by which he meant
a dog which suggests
pit bull
or properly an English
Staffordshire Bull Terrier
thus indicating underclass
being damned souls
hence the devil
specifically Belial
finally signifying
at one remove
someone thinking of
or looking upon
that demon
in London
from the gallery
of Tower Bridge.

All the important people
found this fascinating.

Please Note

To this generation has been given
        many signs
        paper signs.
Paper signs taped to marble pillars,
Plastered to brushed aluminum door frames,
Peeling off thick glass foyer walls
Whose original, hand lettered information
Has been superseded.
Paper signs turning beautiful atria into
        bulletin boards; majestic columns
        into telephone poles; our few attempts
        at grandeur into the image of every family's
        refrigerator door.
Paper signs modifying the traffic pattern
        our architects designed
Paper signs replacing the receptionist
        who was not cost-effective
Paper signs papering over the flaws
        in our forethought
Announcing the bake sales, candy drives,
        cookie campaigns, auctions, golf outings,
        walks, trots, canters, and runs,
        bingo evenings and casino nights
        and all the baffling array of raffles
        we employ to move money to the places
        it ought simply have gone
        in the first place.
Paper signs telling me, for certain,
        that the Space Station will never
        fly, that we will not plan
        to save the ecosphere before the

autopsy, that poverty will be ever
a business tool and never a
quaint memory, that we will
never be able to resist building
the button to which we will
affix the note "Do Not Push"
relying on the tape to hold,
the operator to read,
the language to be the
right one for the
occasion.

Hello

If you leave a message
after the beep
it will be immediately inscribed
phonetically
in cuneiform
on clay tablets
which will be baked
and then secretly buried
in an archeological site
in Turkey.

Your message
will also be translated
into Tibetan, Arabic and Classical Mayan
and painted onto silk banners
by expert calligraphers
who will present them to us
in a touching ceremony
when next
we check our messages.

It will be a glorious event
and our only regret
is that
you won't be there
to see it.

But please
do your part
the essential part
by leaving a message
after the beep.

Looking at This Streetscape

The wires and cables
draping over the intersection.

The hot asphalt streets,
double stripe of cowardice
down their strong,
sticky backs.

The mailboxes,
green
and blue.

The sidewalks,
the pedestrian staircases,
the manhole covers shielding
an intricate veinery
of sewers, water pipes, steam trunks
and gas lines.

This woof and warp
of our connection.

One would hardly imagine
that we have such trouble
getting along, maintaining civility.

That we should invent the telephone
only to throw it across the room
is too much of our story.

The Influence of Pigeons on Architecture

No ledges, no protruding ornament,
no scrollwork, bas-relief,
no cunning recesses.
No gargoyles glaring from above,
created just to spit, to vomit,
and betweenwhiles, to watch.

No niches, with or without
statues of saints,
no statues of saints
or generals or famous citizens.
Perhaps, because no statue:
no actual saints, famous generals,
widely respected citizens.

Carefully maintained roosting boxes
for peregrine predators.

The old and ornamental
booby-trapped with spikes,
draped in screens, the caltrops,
scarps and curtains of Art's
long battle against Nature.
Faux owls and ersatz snakes,
summoning Minerva and Satan
to the contest.

The new struts and flaunts
such boring uniformity

that small brains find no landmark
remember nothing moments
after passing, moments after searching
for anything to grasp.

Do They Still Pick Rags in My Old City?

What's that?
  I say looking out my car window
  at him
  bending, shaking,
    searching, choosing even there
  beside the trash-filled
    empty field
picking rags in my old city.
Do they still pick rags in my old city?
I had not thought it;
and having passed
may soon forget
again.

Even the Crippled

Even the cripples in Pittsburgh
are in better shape.
Already eighteen steps above the sidewalk
when I saw her,
hands clutching each rail
determined
eight steps still to go.
Resting, before the final assault,
head and shoulders bent
into the assault of time.

At the top, waiting,
her walker.

Sentinels

The snowpersonages,
the
snowgentlefolk
have blossomed on the lawns
again.

Whence they come is unknown.
Oh, I have seen
children,
and a few adults,
rolling snow into balls
as though to counterfeit
the snowcitizenry, but their efforts
only impersonate
the real thing: the oddly-dressed,
intriguingly-formed
true snowpeople
who keep an eye on the children
and have that understated air of calm
and good will
that mere snow statues
would never be
capable of.

At Monteverdi's *Magnificat*

Twenty minutes into the
Magnificat
down the side aisle
came a man,
a Torah cradled
lovingly, dutifully
in the crook of
    his arm
the wrappings showing
over his shoulder, the
two handles
    protruding.

One wonders to see
the Torah processing along
the side aisle
of Calvary Episcopal,
    that Gothic basilica.

The man turned to sit
having reached the transept
putting down his burden,
a daughter,
all in winter wrappings,
the two horns of
her animal-shaped
winter hat
protruding.

So bore this man
his treasure,
the word,
up the side aisle
during the *Fecit potentiam*
of the *Magnificat*.

Carnegie Library, Pittsburgh

Ambulance out front of the library again today
Gurney hustling through the great bronze doors.
Why am I not surprised?
Too many conflicts in all those books
More than some folks can take;
Wars and civil wars
Rapine and rage
Adventure, lust, passion
Distilled to typeface and
Coiled like adders along the shelves.

Where are the health warnings?
Where are the nurses on staff?

The Van

I.

At the university
bookstore
the policy
just announced –
books
to be phased out.

II.

In the museum
of espionage
the teen asked –
You mean, spies
are real?

III.

The van,
the school van,
had, stenciled around
its yellow-orange sides,
a single, narrow strand
of barbed wire.
On the door, it said –
Door Will Not Open

Domain

My kingdom is an archipelago:
this office, a table across the hall,
the basement game room.
A rocking chair on the second floor,
one third of the bed,
the northeast chair
at the kitchen table.

A dozen bookcases,
and all the lands and titles
appertaining thereto.
Their rights and freedoms.

Beyond this, I have arranged,
along with some allies,
for formal gardens and open parkland
in the city, also certain museums
and a scattering of libraries, that I might
never be far from culture
when I step abroad.

Add to this burden
eight square yards of fertile ground
wholly devoted to agriculture.
True wealth, after all, is good land.

Like an Old War Horse

> "Did writers once compare
> some action of remembrance
> to pensioned war elephants
> hearing the phalanx drums?"

Safely in the ground lies the last war horse,
three or four decades now; and more than a century
is gone since any horse, trained to gunpowder,
joined, nostrils flaring, in a proper charge;
but the tired simile still pricks its ears
still trots out at the imagined bugle call,
or metaphorical whiff of black powder,
summoned by we who persistently assert
the lethargy of January molasses
though it runs faster in our heated winters
than it ever could in the near-Arctic
air-conditioned July.

Commandments for July

It's July,
but they've rounded up
the cheerleaders
and put them in
Santa's Helper outfits.
White hooded catsuits.
Lacy, transparent, the openings
lined with alabaster fur.

They are all blonde.
They are representing
headache medicine.

I live in a culture
where young, blonde,
slender, pretty
is a résumé.
A job description.

Thou shalt not deplore it.
Thou probably ought not notice it.
There are competitions,
but, I suspect, thou shalt not
wonder when youngblondeslender
will be an Olympic sport.

Thou shalt not suggest
that Christie's handles the auction
when they go private.

Thou shalt drop the Calvinist bifocals,
my friends insist.
Youngblondeslender is a virtue,
they say, like charity,
or a wicked curveball.
Only coroners
really judge people
by what's inside.

No Solicitors #1

> After a sign, remembered
> by my wife, in Quincy, IL.
> "No Solicitors
> No Jehovah's Witnesses"

No Solicitors
No Jehovah's Witnesses
No masterless samurai
No Vandals, and no Visigoths
No Ostrogoths, no Alans, no Marcomanni

No false prophets
No followers of false prophets
No friends of followers of false prophets
No literary critics

No hostage-taking space aliens
No demons
No haughty angels
No desert djinn, unless in original packaging

No world conquerors
No one who doesn't wear a watch
No one who dislikes Dickens
No one who thinks of Italian cooking
    as spicy

**customer
parking
only**

It is decreed that one has only
45 minutes to rent your video
and get some coffee
while parked in this lot,
before you must move on;

so what I need:

a car that can go on home
without me
so that my limited social interactions
might last an hour,
(If our Lord's disciples
are parked at Starbucks,
he'll come back from the Garden
and find himself flat out of luck,
apostleless on the Allegheny Plateau)

so what we need:

a robot that will cheaply,
but persistently, seek out the
gates of Eden and signal their location,
maybe slip past the Cherubim
and bring back a slice of fruit
from the other tree
so that we might have time
and scope for some real

personal relationships
which, frankly, just isn't going to
happen without more eons in an age,
and anyway, with that kind
of car and that kind of robot
I can see the future opening with
possibility

but I am allowed one coffee
and then I,
and my co-dependent vehicle,
must take a movie home
to experience its dreams
rather than
my own.

Squirrel Hill, Saturday

The clerk in the post office
gives me one penny in change,
says Don't spend it all in
one place.

I think how expensive
it will be to comply,
the foreign currency,
the international postage.

The bookstore panhandler
specifies Eight dollars
Eight dollars.

A girl, two years old,
refuses to leave the window.
Her family is stepping away,
calling We're leaving
but it's not working.
The father's shoulders drop
in defeat, he turns his back,
departing says Write
when you get work.

A Break for Freedom in the 61C Cafe

She and her lion
made a run for it,
but her dad nabbed her
at the door.

Imagination conjures the future
she just lost: wandering
the interstices of Squirrel Hill,
feral child and feral plush
wise in the ways
of semi-residential
urban landscapes.

She will know the scent
of caterers anywhere,
will know how to slip
a pizza out of the delivery
guy's rack, unseen.
The lion will prowl for
unattended toy sheep, lost dolls;
will snack on yappy little dogs.

I presume she'll fashion
doeskin bikinis for warm weather,
make winter cloaks
of pilfered fox stoles, stitched
with discarded mink collars.

Her mother is torn between
loss and secret admiration.
She trusts the lion.

Superman Behind the Counter

I point at the logo
on his chest, the blazoned S.

"Aren't you supposed to change,"
I ask, "before you come to work?"

"Awww," he says.
"I don't care anymore."

All The Important People #7

You would understand the layout
better, if, knees complaining,
you climbed the dusty, ill-kept steps
of the south bell tower and
careful of the pigeon droppings
lest you go blind, looked out.
But there is no tower,
nor cathedral, nor chapel, nor church,
and on the streets no dogs
being walked, and most particularly
not any Welsh corgis whatsoever
nor are the residents forthcoming,
nor the maps accurate despite
being meticulous and delicately elaborate.
There must be a bell tower,
surely, the place is so near Bristol
and the sea.
A further detail is that
all the important people
are elsewhere.

Nature, Suffering by Comparison

The azaleas blossomed in the glowing pink
    of a Baskin-Robbins spoon,
    though not as durably.
After the flowers fell it was
    the same green, month after month,
    the green the Paris designers liked so much
    a year ago,
    then dropped at the end of the season.

Insidious

Don't even try to tell me
that volcanoes don't know
exactly what they are doing;
surrounding themselves
with the richest soil, simmering
with nutrients; lifting
their shoulders into the sun
at the perfect angle for vineyards
and olive groves; enticing
with saunas, hot springs, mud baths,
and promises of health; poking
out of the sea and disingenuously tempting
people to settle down.
Getting folks dependent on them
and then indulging
in a tantrum; throwing
a spectacular fit;
or maybe just quietly filling hollows
with asphyxiating gas;
pretending to be god-like
in fury, while sending out
that pathetic psychopathic subtext
that challenges us
to stop them
before they kill again.

Don't give me that
Forces-of-Nature bullshit
or some crap about a deity's
mysterious ways.
I know pathology

when I see it: self-centered,
self-destructive, calculating.
Volcanoes know perfectly well
what they are doing.

Armageddon

Is it when the trees are slaughtered?

Is it when children cower
under the kitchen stairs?

Is it when
one says to the other
"Just drive over him" or

is it not until
the same phrase
is shouted?

Or is it not until
the car moves
that one finally rises
from the porch chair
understanding that the Enemy
has come
the barbarians
are at the wall
and it is time to go inside
walk to the telephone
and finally
raise the alarm?

On Visiting the Dying Suburban Mall

The bookstore, and the colleague
I came for
gone.

I think of basilicas, the Roman
shopping malls,
dead,
turned into churches.
And there is a church, here,
moved into one
of the empty
slots.

Why am I always turning to Rome
and Greece
for comfort
and answers?
They killed their best
for being best.
Their bookstores are all closed
too.

If you build it,
they will eventually
forget why.

It's All Time-Machines, She Said

It's all time-machines,
She said.

And I imagined
A cottage industry;
Every suburban garage with
One up on cinderblocks.

A revival of brass fittings,
Of scrimshaw decoration, intaglio accessories
(So we arrive in the future
With aesthetic values in plain sight)

Popping brews, stoking
Weber® kettles, polishing the chronorotor,
And discussing which decades
Look good this year.

Kids,
She said,
Books, laws, buildings, ideas
That will go into the Future;

We're putting our stamp
On it now,
She said.
It's all time-machines.

III

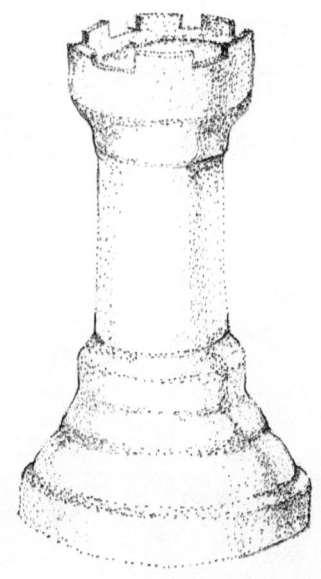

For Love, This Cup

The sun has come again, fingers searching,
skimming across the ocean, the shore,
the ridge to the east, and now this cup,
illustrated with a ship bearing
Helen toward Troy, or is it
Aeneas outbound from Carthage?
I forget which; but already the light
has lost interest and moved on west
over the river, into the greener,
not yet ripening, fields.

I really do wonder where you are;
whether this dawn will find you
on the surface, or only trace the ground
you are beneath; whether it will
bring out the old shadows
on your face, betray anything about your hopes,
betray the passage of time
since I, for love, offered the whole world
and you took it.

Stipulated Conditions

We had kissed once, briefly.
She wanted separate bedrooms.

I am wondering about holding hands
hoping for a third date
but she is in final negotiations.

She lists her conditions.
Separate bedrooms.
Our vacations separate
as well, so that
the relationship will stay fresh.

I am hearing this message that says
NO
but she thinks she is saying:
YES.
Big-time yes.

We have exchanged one kiss.
No more than four seconds. Less.

Also on the list is this guy
who comes to town
every few months.
She needs to explore
that relationship, see
where it will go.

We have kissed only once.
Briefly.

Postulate #5

In her world parallel lines
went on and on
never meeting.

They wanted to meet,
often desperately,
but just *wouldn't*.

They had so much
in common.
But no.

The Origin of a Long, Bitter Story

A trick of the ear,
the shape of a lobe,
or nerves galled tender
too young to know.

She spent her lifetime
hearing
what others meant
only for themselves.

Follies

In the gardens of her memory
she has erected
ruins.

Beyond the ancient catalpa,
a broken tower
signifies a grand affair,
that was
in life
only a smile, one afternoon,
and perhaps a wink.

Turning at the fountain,
crossing the canal,
behold the slope to the right
topped by the ashes
and eternal flame
of the Portico to the Unknown Lover,
a cenotaph.

Over here are three grottoes
in memory of men
she spurned without a word,
but the inscriptions
assure us of their long
secret devotion.

The intended effect
is studied desolation.

A triumphant,
even voluptuous,
pathos.

Hair

I assume
she leaves
that oval patch
at the top
of her head
un-dyed
so that God
will recognize her
for who she is.

Awkward Stage

Serious Keltic male, 16,
raised American
seeks responsible,
compassionate, wise,
attentive
tutelary deity;
whom oak trees must be
sacred to
(with a differing aspect
related to each major variety)
but can also be present
in erratic boulders resting
at the edge of pastures;
annual death a minus,
no bigots, no chauvinists,
no hypocrites leaning on the
occasional miracle to patch things
up,
must have respect for truth;
and no self-satisfied
self-centered
unmoved movers
need apply.

Would I Give the World, All of It, for Love?

All the world? Of course, why not?
Who would not give two worlds – Pluto, say,
And Uranus for a glass of melon juice
On any desert summer day?

But should I give the world, this world,
To you? Perhaps you would merely spend it,
Or put it aside, as you did once with my heart
To say only afterwards, the light fading
Into a chill evening, "I forgot."
It is not for me that I tremble,
That I hesitate, but for the world.

93 Lines Wasted

Okay, let's say I'm writing this poem
and it's about
you.

And I, being a poet,
want it to be universal;
so it can't be a paean
to your virtue, because
the only universal virtue
this poem is likely to find
in its readers
is a basic, possibly quite limited,
literacy.

So this poem is going to be
about what you'll wish I
hadn't delved into, isn't it?
It's going to be about how
you tried, but didn't measure up.
Except you didn't try all that hard,
did you? It was more a case of
thinking about trying, and then giving up,
isn't it? Of having, somewhat sincerely,
meant to try.

I know the feeling, but this poem
isn't about me,
it's about you.
And this, right here,
if I were a popular poet,
is the point,

where I would let you off the hook,
sneak in a hidden compliment,
hold out a dollop of honey and a bit of hope;
but I'm another kind of poet
today
and besides, this is about you,
and I'm fairly certain that
there's been too much undeserved honey
and too many easy exits
in your life.

So let's take a risk here,
and see if we can delve into the
Plutonic depths, though I can see that you've
never gone beyond the shallows of the depths
(and spare me the simple moments of despair,
and the twelve step programs,
and the self-righteousness about how you've known
the depth of your inadequacy, because inadequacy
is not only a self-fulfilling prophecy, and an
excuse, and a given, and not all that interesting –
but concentrating on it is
a stupid, narcissistic infinite loop
for the mind to get into
rather than actually seeking self
knowledge)

(which you knew perfectly well
without me telling you)

and let's just see if
you can find something
down there worth knowing
worth bringing out at the
cost of killing your current,
let's face it,
totally hodgepodge
substitute for a real
personality.

And I'm not talking about bringing
forth the lost beloved,
entire and whole,
if only you can keep
from looking back,
because the beloved is gone
whether you look or you don't
so forget that.

I'm sensing resistance.
I'm getting a vibe,
right through the paper
or the screen, or the air,
or however this is reaching you
that you'd rather not.

You'd rather read about somebody else
taking the journey.
You'd rather see

the thing done metaphorically
while you sit with your popcorn
stinking up the darkness
at the cineplex.

Isn't that it?

Typical.

And to think
I went to the trouble
of writing this whole poem
all the previous ninety lines
about

You.

What I Learned

What I learned from
        that relationship
is to crush the
restaurant saltines
in the package,
        before you open it.

Also, that when
        all the signs
        are saying
        Stay Away:

Stay away.

What She Was

She was like a pneumonia,
        taking my breath away,
        leaving me feverish;
And she was a bursitis,
        making me weak in the knees;
A hay fever,
        bringing tears to my eyes.
An obsessive-compulsive disorder,
        I thought only of her,
        acted only for her.
An anaphylactic reaction,
        she made me sweaty,
        and rash.
She was amnesia,
        but don't ask me why.
She was Lou Gehrig's Disease,
        scoring her own extra bases
but always putting me out
        at first.
She was the common cold,
        and everybody got her,
        recurrently.
She was kleptomania;
        she took everything.
And then she was gonorrhea,
        or, at any rate,
        she was gone.

In sum, she was the Black Death,
>   and I was Europe:
>   devastated.

In The Whole History Of Time?

Has anyone
ever
standing in the ruins of a
collapsed relationship
said to themselves:
It was
my fault. It was
all
my fault.

The Progressive

It will be delivered when I need it
whether I want it or not.

It will be accurate
despite my preference for euphemism.

Seductive, it will engage
my reluctant attention.

Adapted just for me
it will teach, it will educate.

It will expect me
to sharpen my vocabulary.

It will slowly tease me
into learning languages.

I will feel proud
to have faced a difficult truth.

Each issue will prod me to wisdom
and away from error.

There will be only one personal ad.
The right one.

Eyes, This Big

He is telling a story,
and she is listening.
He says, "Your eyes gets this big."
and makes a cartoon face.
He is telling a story, all animation,
and she is listening.
He is telling a story, all animation,
and she, twenty years younger, is listening.
He says, "Your eyes gets this big."
and makes a cartoon face.
He, graying, is telling a story,
and she, twenty years younger, is listening.
The words are accurate, but the tune
is in the modifications.
How if I said: He, graying, is
telling a story, all animation,
and she, twenty years younger, is listening eagerly?
Something is alive between these two,
but here is my film-noir lens:
my light oasis midnight coffee shop;
fade in; the shadows are unnaturally sharp;
he is telling a story, all animation,
the inner collar of his jacket is maroon,
with one 50s-ish white stripe;
she, twenty years younger, in a hooded
patchwork sweater, is listening.
This image, too, is accurate,
but what you see is not.
My words mislead.
He is telling a story.
She is listening.

Family

I take this lesson from the family of planets:
    That each child may take its own way,
    Yet still orbit the same parent.
    And that, perhaps, over time
    The eccentricities will slowly decrease,
        the orbits gradually harmonize,
    Though it may take
    a very, very long time.

I give them, though, this warning:
    Leave, before it is too late.
    Before the cold,
        the aimlessness
        and lost momentum.
    Leave.
    Before your parent destroys you.

"But will they come when you do call for them?"
—Henry IV, part I, III, 1

They did not come
my parents
for the beatings
or the bully who threatened
hurling me into traffic.

Play in the back
they said.

Nor for the mouse
cowering on the stairs
or the car sliding
into the street.

No it's not
they said.

But my second grade teacher
took *Oliver Twist*
would not give it back
lest I be discouraged
and cleave not to Dick and Jane.

Oh then

like lions from Mt. Atlas
like avenging angels

like very Huns on horseback
did they come.

I remember from the hall
the roars in that room
pitied her
my teacher
wondered if she would live.

They came
my parents
for words for reading
for what was important
for Charles Dickens
they came.

It is enough.

Photonic Relationships

The newspaper said that photons were entangled
And messages can now be sent faster than light.
Despite what Einstein said;
Despite what Bohr said.
But what my brother said.

I thought the article begged more questions
than it claimed to answer:
Wasn't "photon entanglement" presuming the consequent?
And how could they rule out artifacts
of measurement?
But my brother said, Don't you see the
paradox? Don't you see the answer?

So I started in with logic,
with my suspicion that quarks are only
our era's very tiny
epicycles within epicycles…

But my brother said,
Space and Time are irrelevant.
There are not two photons,
but one thing only.
Tweak it here, and it moves there,
instantaneously,
only because
it is One.
Despite what Einstein said.
Despite what the paper said.

We live six hundred miles apart,
The better part of an hour
at the speed of sound.
Three point two two thousandths of a second
at the speed of light.
We don't talk often,
and see each other less.
But my brother says,
Space and Time
are irrelevant.

Not For Love, But Something Else

Not for love would I give
the world; love is cheap
when you come down to it, and
we so inevitably come down to it
while at the same time
love can cost you far more than
a mere world, even when you
don't make an offer, never sign the contract,
never even get to put in a bid
that the auctioneer would notice.

But for that word, that phrase,
the melody, the song,
the analogy, the perfect metaphor
which lures love, or revives it,
or pins it to the wall for all to know,

That, that formula,
would be worth the world
and more.

IV

Lines Written to an Unknown Audience, Waiting for the Night's First Act

Outside the sky is lowering the lights
to fit the evening mood.
Inside the early drinks
the ones you can still taste
are in hand, as are the cigarettes.

The problem for me, writing this poem,
is that I don't know
anything about you,
where you are reading this
or hearing this.

By the time I do know, it will
be too late to adjust,
to personalize this poem;
the die cast, and tonight's acts
behind us both.

It is an evening for embracing
the little deaths: the drinks,
the cigarettes, these lines,
the gap between me, at this table,
already in your past, and you.

The Alcoholic Beverages of India

The name Arrack
tells nothing
of how the stuff
tastes

Just as the word
whiskey
gives no idea –
smell of burning crofts –
of the range of it
nor really
does the formula –
centuries of pain –
for arrack

Words have only meanings
that one already knows
or thinks one knows
and mystery –
Sura, Pali, Pendhā,
Andhra Pradesh Kallu –
from what we suspect

Language needeth
one more power
needeth to summon
the thing it names
the very thing
for then it can tell
finally

what you
did to him
and how it was
all my fault

Not Feeling That Lucky, Seeking

after Billy Collins

So I was
power-using
Google Metaphor searches
because my life
is
the Red Fort of Delhi
and most especially
because my perspective
is not just *like*
the Bhadon,
with its scalloped arches,
but *is* pavillionated
in Bhadonitude
chiefly
in contrast to
its mirror,
Sawan.

But this engine
wants my life
to be
the Seneca Red Sandstone Quarry
which it
most definitely
is *not*,
neither is it
the right panel
of Plate 24

from Maximilian's
Ehrenpforte
despite the griffin,
the armor,
the tympanic membranes
that gave me such trouble
as a child.

The metaphor
that is given
is best left
still wrapped
still beribboned
in the bench
under the coatrack.

New Labels on Old Jars

I was reading Caesar's *Commentaries
on the Gallic War*, which has always
for centuries
been Caesar's *Commentaries on the Gallic War*
but now
it's suddenly
stupidly
The Conquest of Gaul.

So I'm thinking the next edition
of Shakespeare
might be
Five-Act Entertainments for the Globe.

And the Gideons
will be putting
A People Ran out of Eden
in every hotel room drawer,
along with Homer's
A Sulk Turns Sour.

I had already decided
that Pittsburgh
should be Chathamopolis,
but still I dither
between a new name
for myself
and
actual change.

Famous Poet, Rant, Point of Order

I'm here in the dark
and the poet
is reading
this rant
about the war,
it doesn't matter which,
people were dying,
and the poet
is against war
and this particular war
and so am I
but this is the true story
of some friend
who went and came back,
told these lurid tales
to all his –
take your pick –
beat, hippie, boho, outsider
friends, the poet's friends,
and every word is bull,
after training camp, at least,
but what do you say?
Here in the dark
I look around,
the dim light highlighting
the henna in the hair
of every second college girl,
their heads are nodding,
they're eating this up
that's just how it was
and so are the guys

and the poet
is at the part
where the friend's unit
gets abandoned in central Siberia
and they have to walk out
and I'm thinking about facts,
about the Czech Legion, who really were
abandoned in Siberia
and cut their way out
and *that* story is gripping
and ugly and horrible
and also *true*,
but what do you say?

Here in the dark
I'm telling myself
it shouldn't matter,
think of it as fiction,
and the poet
is naming names, famous names
among poets,
real names of the friends
this ex-soldier – who may
have been through hell
or may have been a clerk –
piled all these lies on,
and I'm dodging the insult
to our intelligence
by imagining someone
bursting up from the audience

raising an Objection, or a Point of Order,
hauling forty or fifty reference books
onto the stage, plugging in a laptop
right there and getting the facts straight,
looking up this old friend's record
telling myself it's the emotion
that matters, not the poet's
lack of experience, lack of judgment,
inability to distinguish crap and compost,
and after all
what do you say?

Post-reading I'm hanging out in the dark
of the cheapest nearby bar
and the poet
isn't here, the reception
being black tie,
but the unknown poets
are here, kicking around
the lies the poet of the evening
told, putting an extra spin,
a telling biographical detail,
on the latest version,
and I'm thinking that they
are citizens of the Republic
responsible for electing
the most powerful government
on the planet
and ought to be trading in truth
or in facts, at least,

and not in fourth-hand
cheap-jack frauds,
but what do you say?

At the Mountain Inn, Shaded by Broken Pines

How can you say
it's poem time?
The fog has not
yet settled
in the mountain pass,
our horses
still steam and nicker
in the stable yard.

How can you call
for poem time
when we have not found
the weapons that surely
tumbled over the ridge?

There are buttons
to be sewn back on,
crops untended,
and my memorandum
to His Highness
on the status of
our frontier.

We still do not know
what happened.
We do not know why,
or what it meant,
not even who
was the hero.

It cannot yet
be poem time.

14 Lines

But why do you do it?
You don't even like poetry,
not what they do these days
anyway.

Because, mostly, one needs
a whole field of wheat
the scything of the wheat
the stacking, the thrashing,
the flailing, the milling,
the thorough drying, the mixing
with yeast, and beer, and careful
baking – each step, and all the process –

but sometimes one just wants
a shot of whiskey, neat.

In Each of Our Wallets

My wallet tells me that AAA
    will ride to my rescue
that the Union will stand beside me
that someone will pay my medical bills
that I have Social Security.

I can drive legally.
I can play in a
    World Shogi Federation tournament,
    a United States Chess Federation tournament,
    a Fédération Internationale des Échecs tournament,
    or get two free games of miniature golf
    at Wildwood Acres Family Retreat.

Some of the contents of my wallet
    can legally defray, if tendered,
    all debts, public and private,
though you'd have trouble convincing
    my old lovers of that.

I am writing this poem, almost talking to myself,
    while the street person at the next table
    note-paper spread in front of him
    is talking to himself.
It is hard to feel utterly confident
    that there is a distinct line between us.

The line between us being, after all,
    the pieces of paper, the scraps of plastic,
    in each of our wallets.

Their relative credibility.
The meaning that society has agreed to assign
    each of them, and by extension, to us.

Blockbuster will rent me a video, if
    it has been censored to their tastes.
The Central Blood Bank will take my platelets, if
    my new diagnosis fits their profile.
The bank will give me cash, if
    I ask for less than I gave them.
The Living Will Registry will describe, if called,
    the precise bargain I would make with death.

Nudge

Some months ago, I sent to thee,
several poems, thusly named
[herein place their titles]
hoping they
like Roman legions would march through
the dark forests of your slush
and conquer. But now, like Augustus,
I beat my head against the wall
calling for Varus and my eagles,
distraught by the silence which is all
that has come back since they left here.

Do not force me to find
the literary equivalent of a Germanicus,
and send him unto [herein place the publication's name],
scourging thee for thy inaction
to pillage and search thy land
for, metaphorically, my eagles,
which is to say, plainly,
the poems you have still not read.
Take this envelope, addressed to me,
well-stamped and adequate,
and use it honorably for a fit reply.
Elsewise, be thou warned, just one month hence
I'll call them back,
or know the reason why.

Deadline

I see the contest deadline
was the first
and it is now the fifth
so I was wondering if by the first
you meant the first
or instead
the *whole* of February?

I note also that you will not take
submissions by express mail or by e-mail
and I assume that by express mail you include
the Pony Express among others
which I well understand, because the horses
can make a mess under the porte-cochère
but in this case I will have sent the story
from this house by sedan chair
to my neighbor's
and they will ride it into town
on their Tennessee Walker,
not an express horse at all,
and only then will it be scanned and e-mailed
to you
so though you will have received it by e-mail
I will not have sent it by e-mail
and I trust that you can recognize
the difference.

While your rules
regarding theme and length
are quite definite, still
I am sure you will agree

true Art has long ago discarded
the requirements of form, of subject
and of anything inhumanly restrictive
so I have taken these as suggestions,
and while good suggestions in their way
have had to put them aside
in this particular case.

Finally, when you receive my submission –
I await only your kind permission –
you will note that it consists
of key passages only, those scenes
that express the essence of the piece
because we both understand
that time is valuable
and inspiration more so
and one can hardly be expected to write out
an entire story without the assurance
of already having won the contest
so I have completed sufficient material
for you to judge the thing
imagining for yourselves the parts that I have left
as I say
to the imagination.

May I assume that no
technicalities
will bar my entry
from consideration?

in kiva han

I should be correcting
a manuscript
but found, in my bag,
only the empty envelope
cleverly having forgotten
to stuff it
before I left the house.

This poem should be entitled
Cenotaph
or some Greek term for
empty envelope
and this stanza would connect
today's incident to
universals of experience,
to bodies after death, to decorous
ruins.

But such a poem
should be left
to a better observer than
I,
who came into town
this morning to find the
typewriter supply store
torn down, along with the coffee
shop and another store I can't remember
and in its place
a parklet.

The Latest Literary Device

Your poetry will be more
concise
with the Hyperparnassian Automatic
point-and-shoot
Metaphorizer!

What you write:

>"tree
>   tree
>   tree
>   tree, tree
>   tree"

What you get:

> [the Catalpa in which you first found love, cut down]
> [the Pomegranate where Adonis bled, betrayed]
> [the Pipal that shielded the Waking vision, lost]
> [the Cherries honoring our Republic, sick and
>   withered]
> [the tree on which the Messiah dies],[the Oak of
>   sacrifice for Lake Nemi's King]
> [the choice of the first tree to be planted on Mars]

or

> [the tree of the Knowledge we sorely need;
>   forbidden, if not mythical]

[the Yggdrasill that bound the Earth as one;
    replaced by an imaginary pole]
[the ancient Laurel from a single branch of which
    the Space Shuttle Daphne's bow ornament was
        carved;
    torn apart for souvenirs]
[the Treaty Oak of Texas; poisoned],[the Parliament
    Oak; dead]
[the Christmas tree brought home each year
    grudgingly
        by your father,
            who believes in neither
                god nor man;
            dying]

Buy it now,
and put new meaning
in your work!!!

Poetry Defined

Poetry
is an affectation
of those who
not only
can't fill the page,
they can't
even get the line all the way across.

I Really Think Sela Ward Should Have Dropped the String of Pearls and the Coral Lipstick and the Whole Suburban Goddess Shtick and Gone with Sheer Glamour and *Femme Fatale*, Infuriating Other Women and Turning Men into Slavering Puddles of Meaningless Meat; but This Poem Isn't about Her Anyway

This is not a poem with an epigraph
from García Lorca, because the Lorca epigraphs
have been all used up, and
this is not a poem with an epigraph
from Neruda, as, really, both those
gentlemen deserve to have their
every line for themselves.

This is not a poem "after" another poet
though it is after all the poems
that came before
not to mention most that will come
after.

This is not my poem which says
chess is death
but which doesn't say
that though chess is death
many of its moves
can be beautiful.

This is not my poem on
what the white whale means

and it is not a poem
about George Washington's
despicable land dealings
and not a poem
honoring the American Spirit
through the metaphor
of locomotive smoke stack spark arrestors.
This is not a poem
even mentioning Walt Whitman
or pretending that the East River
is a river
or a poem that caters to the
provincial self-congratulation
of those islands off the coast
at the mouth of the Hudson
because the truth is that
America happens on the mainland
and New York is filled with people
who lacked the courage
to come all the way ashore.

This is not my poem with the long title
about Sela Ward
nor my poem about the girl who
made me choose between her
and my teddy bear
nor my poem about the woman
who set off all my alarms
before she even came around
the corner

or the woman whose primary
question about Delphi
was the quality of the shopping
there.

This might be a poem
about things being defined
by what they are not
but it isn't a poem using
phrases like negative space
and it isn't a poem
about the divisibility
of paramecia
and it isn't a purple
cow poem
or even a list poem
or a skaldic verse
or a poem about
not being what
might have been.

Lurking at the center
though
is the old dragon, or
what remains of the dragon,
and the awesome question
of what comes
of setting forth
to kill it.

You Must Not Be Taken In

The voice of this poem is not
my voice
but the voice of a narrator
invented, wholly imagined
for the occasion
so you must not be taken in
despite the personal details
the narrator might mention:
the awkward, shy redhead loved and lost;
the seabed town on the continental shelf;
the incongruous silliness of a certain cat named Bastet;
the five casual murders;
the years with the CIA.
But, of course, the narrator
I invented, so
the voice of the poem,
despite all the necessary disclaimers,
is, you should be aware,
my voice.

Rubaiyat LXXI, Revised

The moving finger writes; and, having writ,
moves back, scores out,
rewrites, and having writ,
scores out again, rewords, reworks,
despairs, and starts again,
and pauses, gathers wits, writes,
and having writ,
hesitates, considers, and, unsatisfied,
moves on.

My Play

It was my play
but someone else
was writing the words.

She was right there
and all it needed
was a thoughtful line
confirming her, and
revealing all that
I could be;

but earlier scenes
with other characters
demanded a repeated
pattern.
"You can't show a
deep wound in the first
Act, and not use it."

A happy ending would
have been trivial, I am told.
Good taste insists sincere
emotions end in tragedy.

It was my play,
but somehow I
wasn't writing the words.

Linguistic Changes to Look For

Certain terms should begin to decline in use —
dawn, sunrise, dusk, suntan —
and then drift in meaning.

It will be interesting to track
which words simply fade, and which
gain an ironic edge, at first,
then a nostalgic romanticism.

Likewise the names of all the chlorophyllic plants
should slip in frequency, and then
drift, too, in meaning.

Expect proverbs to contain these lexical items
long after the names have become meaningless
in their primary context.

There was a recent report
of "Moses among the bulrushes"
in a context that implied toreadors
in the Spanish arena.

This is only the beginning.

Cogmire

There are an infinite
number of words
in the English language.

Miserably few of them
make sense.

Every century we claw
a double handful
into meaning.

Each century
many fall away.
We've lost *bansheewrapper*
somehow
in all its flavors,
and *cogmire*;
was it a noun
or a verb?

Why even
pick up a brush,
with such a paltry
palette?

How bereft
the tongue
without even
cogmire
in useable
condition.

To Demur

I would have the sound
of the grinding
in that same stanza,
and I need hard surfaces,
and I disagree completely.

I would neither add,
nor take away, but
only summon the inner
to emerge more luminously,
with clarity, and luster,
probably using Latinate words,
and some Greek derivations,
for as I have told you
before
there is no poetry in English.

The universal, in the next stanza,
should be more particular.
Here, too, the utter perfection of my dissent
from previous opinions
cannot be overstated.

The fact that I missed
the reference to Schiaparelli
is regrettable; raises some
interesting questions,
questions about line breaks,
about ocelots, and gambits declined,
and, though it might be presumptuous to say so,
the odor of cheap, old aspirin.

Appropriate Salutations

Elephants are best addressed
in iambic pentameter,
Dogs in skaldic kennings,
But cats
will only deign to hear
heroic alexandrines
dripping with servile regret,
though a plate of fish
often says
what no verse
can.

Concise Credo

Words have power.
Even these words.
Even these.

About the Author

Timons Esaias is a poet, satirist, essayist, and writer of short fiction. His works have been published in nineteen languages and have appeared in markets ranging from *5AM, Willard & Maple, Barbaric Yawp* and *Connecticut Review* to *Asimov's Science Fiction* and *Elysian Fields Quarterly: The Literary Journal of Baseball*. His short story "Norbert and the System" has appeared in a textbook and in college curricula. "Shift Change" was a finalist for the British Science Fiction Award. He teaches at Seton Hill University, in the Writing Popular Fiction MFA Program.

Timons has lived in Pittsburgh for about a third of a century, off and on; with stints in St. Louis and in Rantoul, Illinois. He learned to proofread and edit upside-down and backwards, handsetting type from a California case, in the family's basement print shop. (At that same age, he was reading Dick and Jane.) He reads more than is probably good for him, sometimes in languages that have long ago died. His interests include chess, aikido, maritime history and military history. People who know him are not surprised to learn that he lived in a museum for eight years.

He collects chess sets and elephants.

www.ingramcontent.com/pod-product-compliance
Lightning Source LLC
Chambersburg PA
CBHW021127300426
44113CB00006B/327